THIS BOOK BELONGS TO

_____

_____

 LITTLE SIMON

An imprint of Simon & Schuster Children's Publishing Division

1230 Avenue of the Americas, New York, New York 10020

First Little Simon hardcover edition September 2015

Text copyright © 2015 by Laura Schroff

Illustrations copyright © 2015 by Barry Root

LITTLE SIMON is a registered trademark of Simon & Schuster, Inc., and associated colophon is a trademark of Simon & Schuster, Inc.

For information about special discounts for bulk purchases, please contact Simon & Schuster Special Sales at 1-866-506-1949 or business@simonandschuster.com.

The Simon & Schuster Speakers Bureau can bring authors to your live event. For more information or to book an event contact the Simon & Schuster Speakers Bureau at 1-866-248-3049 or visit our website at www.simonspeakers.com.

Designed by Angela Navarra and Chani Yammer

Manufactured in China 0715 SCP

10 9 8 7 6 5 4 3 2 1

ISBN 978-1-4814-1930-7

ISBN 978-1-4814-1931-4 (eBook)

This book has been cataloged with the Library of Congress.

AN INVISIBLE THREAD
CHRISTMAS STORY

By Laura Schroff
and Alex Tresniowski

Illustrated by
Barry Root

LITTLE SIMON
New York   London   Toronto   Sydney   New Delhi

To all the children like Maurice who see
the world from the outside looking in
—L. S.

My name is Maurice,
and I have a friend named Laura.
Some people don't understand how
we can be friends, because we're so
different, but we're great friends.

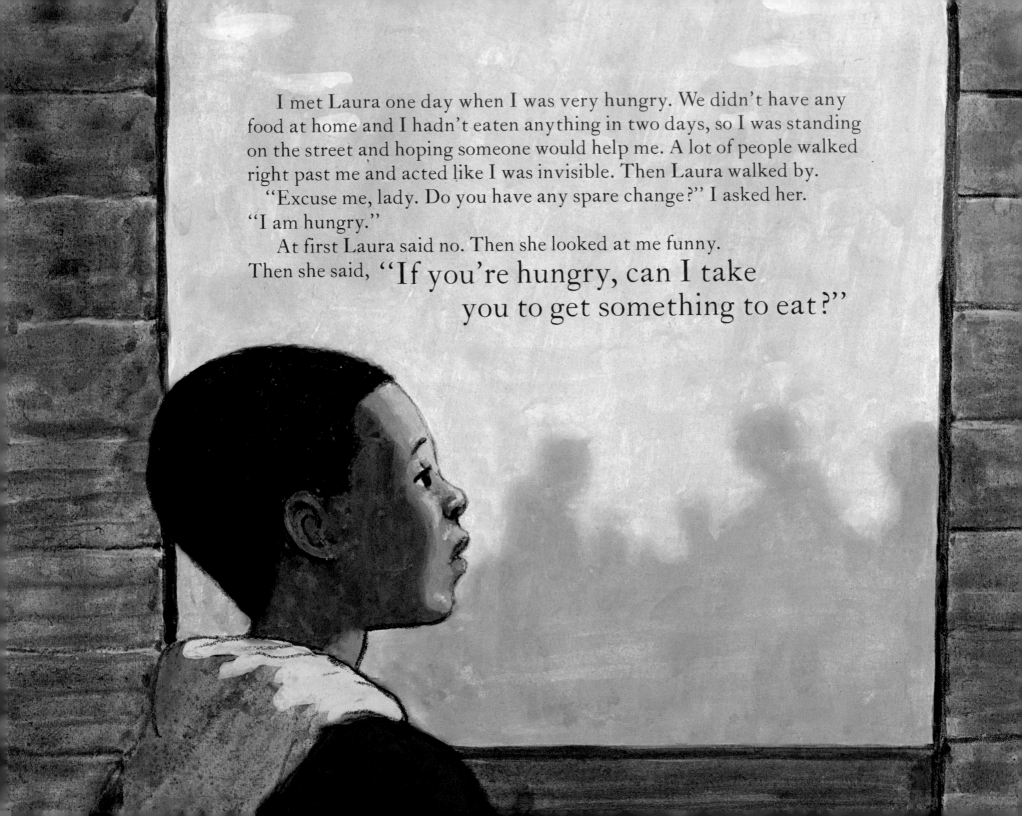

I met Laura one day when I was very hungry. We didn't have any food at home and I hadn't eaten anything in two days, so I was standing on the street and hoping someone would help me. A lot of people walked right past me and acted like I was invisible. Then Laura walked by.

"Excuse me, lady. Do you have any spare change?" I asked her. "I am hungry."

At first Laura said no. Then she looked at me funny. Then she said, "If you're hungry, can I take you to get something to eat?"

I wasn't sure if I should say yes, but then my stomach growled and said, "We're hungry down here. You'd better say yes!" So I told Laura I would go to lunch with her.

I had a cheeseburger and fries and a chocolate milk shake. My stomach and I were both so happy.

Laura could tell I needed a friend and was hungry a lot, so she took me to dinner the next week, and the week after that, and the week after that, too. We had dinner together every Monday night. That's how we became friends.

At one of our dinners, when it was getting colder outside, Laura asked what my plans were for Christmas.

"Nothing," I said.

"Nothing?" she asked. "Do you celebrate Christmas?"

"I know about it," I said. "But we don't have money for toys and things like that. We've never celebrated Christmas."

Laura was surprised.

I told Laura about my family. I had two sisters, a mother, and a grandma, but we didn't have a home. We lived in a small room in a place called a shelter hotel. My mother was sick a lot.

"Have you ever received a Christmas gift?" Laura asked.

"Only once," I said. "Last Christmas I went to a holiday party at the Salvation Army, a place that helps feed people. All the kids there could pick out a present of their very own. A man pointed to a big box of toys and told me I could choose one. I picked out a white teddy bear with a little red heart. It was soft, and sometimes at night when I held it, it made me feel safe. That's the only Christmas gift I ever got," I said.

Laura seemed sad, but then she looked like she had an idea. "Maurice, would you like to spend Christmas with my family and me?" she asked.

I'd seen what Christmas was like for a lot of people on TV. It looked like so much fun. So of course I said, "You bet I would!" I could hardly wait.

The next week I went with Laura to pick out a Christmas tree for the first time. It was so big we almost couldn't carry it back to her apartment, and we had to stop a few times, but we made it.

We decorated the tree in Laura's apartment. Laura showed me how to hang the ornaments, the tinsel, and the lights, too. Then we baked cookies and had hot chocolate. (Baking cookies was one of my favorite things we did on Monday nights. They were always delicious and made the apartment smell so good!)

Then we just sat and looked at the tree all lit up and listened to Christmas carols. It was just like I had seen on TV.

"Maurice, I want you to make a Christmas list so I can give it to Santa," Laura said as we finished eating the cookies.

"You mean I just write it down and Santa brings it?" I asked. That couldn't be true.

"Well, not everything," said Laura, laughing, "but he tries his best."

I couldn't believe it. But I wrote my list and put on it a lot of things that I needed, like a new jacket, scarf, and warm gloves. Then at the very top I wrote what I wanted most of all—a remote control racecar.

I hoped Laura was right about Santa trying to bring a lot of things on the list. Still, I wasn't sure how Santa would find me.

On Christmas Eve, Laura invited me to her apartment again. Her sister Nancy was there too. This time there were a whole bunch of colorful boxes under the tree with bows on them. It was amazing!

"It looks like this red one is for you," said Laura, "and you can open it tonight. It's from me!"

I picked up the box, but I wasn't sure what to do. I looked at Laura, who told me to take off the paper to see what was inside. I had never had a wrapped present before. I tore off the wrapping paper. And . . . it was exactly what I had wanted— a remote control racecar!

That night we had dinner and milk and cookies, and I got to play with my new car and dunk my cookies in my milk. It was the best Christmas Eve I'd ever had.

On Christmas Day I went with Laura and Nancy to their sister's family's house outside the city. I had been there before, but I still couldn't believe how big it was. The yard looked like a whole park to me, covered with snow.

I got to see Laura's father, Nunzie, and her brothers, Frank and Steven, and her sister Annette and Annette's husband, Bruce, and their kids, Colette, Derek, and Brooke. Derek was about my age. I brought my new racecar with me so Derek and I could play.

And then I saw their Christmas tree. . . . It was even bigger than Laura's tree, and underneath there were a million colorful boxes, all wrapped up.

I thought, *This has to be the luckiest family in the world.*

We all sat down for Christmas dinner. Annette said grace. "Dear God," she said. "We thank you for all the wonderful blessings you have given us. And we thank you for letting us spend this Christmas with our new friend, Maurice."

Then we had dinner. We had a big roast and a ham and mashed potatoes and green beans and corn and warm rolls. And that wasn't even everything! I had never seen so much food in my life. But the food wasn't even the best part.

The best part was how everyone sat around the big dining room table and talked and laughed and had so much fun just being together. It felt nice and warm, and everyone was happy. I had never seen that many happy people together before. I hoped someday I could have a family like that too.

After dinner we all sat around the Christmas tree so everyone could open their presents. Colette got a jewelry box. Derek got a basketball. Brooke got a beautiful doll. They got a lot of other presents, and it was fun to watch.

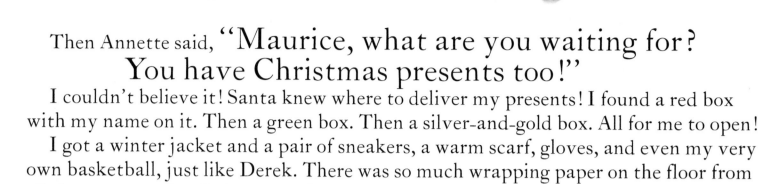

Then Annette said, "Maurice, what are you waiting for?
You have Christmas presents too!"

I couldn't believe it! Santa knew where to deliver my presents! I found a red box with my name on it. Then a green box. Then a silver-and-gold box. All for me to open!

I got a winter jacket and a pair of sneakers, a warm scarf, gloves, and even my very own basketball, just like Derek. There was so much wrapping paper on the floor from all the presents that I almost couldn't see my legs and feet!

Later that night we said good-bye, and Laura drove me home. I'm pretty sure I fell asleep because my stomach was full and my brain was full. And my heart was full too.

When we got back to Laura's apartment, I asked her if I could leave my presents there. I was a little worried that if I took them back to the shelter hotel, they might get lost—or worse.

"Of course," said Laura. "They will be here so you can play with them anytime you visit." I carefully left my remote control car and basketball. I took my jacket, scarf, sneakers, and gloves. But I also left something else.

Laura walked me home.

"Thank you for giving me my first ever real Christmas," I said. "It was very special to me."

"No, Maurice," said Laura. "Thank you for making my Christmas so special by spending it with me." Then she gave me a great big hug.

I waved good-bye as I walked up the steps, and Laura waited for me to go inside. I was carrying a bag of food for my mother, sisters, and grandma so they could have a taste of Christmas too. I wanted to share whatever I had with them.

When Laura got back to her apartment, she noticed I had left something under her Christmas tree.

"I thought we opened all the presents," she said out loud, puzzled. But there was one more, just for her.

It wasn't in a box, and it wasn't wrapped. It was just tucked under the tree, but it was still a Christmas present.

It was the only thing I had to give her, my white teddy bear with the little red heart. *Merry Christmas,* I wrote to Laura on a piece of paper. *Thank you for being my friend.*

That night I went to sleep all
tingly and feeling good. I felt happy and full. I thought
about my wonderful Christmas and what I loved the most.
I didn't love my presents the most, although I loved them very much.
I didn't love the food the most, although I loved that, too.

What I loved the most was my new friends sitting around the big dining room table, laughing and joking and having fun just being together. I thought about how, when I got older, I wanted to have a family too, and sit around the big dinner table with all my kids and laugh and talk and have a lot of special Christmases together.

Just before I drifted off to sleep, I looked outside and saw a silver moon in the sky. It seemed like it was making the whole city glow and twinkle, just like I felt. And I thought, *This was the best Christmas ever.*

Laura sat in front of her Christmas tree, holding her new white teddy bear.
Then she looked out her window and saw the same glowing, sparkly moon in
the sky. She felt the warm glow too. And she thought,
This was the best Christmas ever.

LAURA'S NOTE

I am blessed to still be friends with Maurice, whom I met almost thirty years ago. He was just a kid when I first saw him on the street in New York City, but now he's a proud man and a happy husband and father. His dream of having his own big family, and his own big dining room table, came true. Whenever I can, I sit around that big table with Maurice and his wife, Michelle, and their seven smart, beautiful children. The gift of his friendship is something I'm grateful for every day.

Something else wonderful has come out of our friendship. A few years ago I wrote a book, *An Invisible Thread*, and since then I've been able to share our story with so many people around the world. This has allowed me to share the powerful idea at the heart of our story—how one small act of kindness can change someone's life.

So while we rush around buying gifts, it's my hope this book becomes a reminder of the true meaning of the holidays—the importance of giving from our hearts. If you encourage your children to give from their hearts, I promise you the gift they'll receive in return will be one hundred times more rewarding. One small act of kindness changed my life. It can change yours, too.

Laura Schroff

MAURICE'S NOTE

I remember going to my friend Laura's fiftieth birthday party and standing up to give her a toast. "I was going down the wrong path, and God sent me an angel," I told all the guests. "And that angel was Laura." I wasn't exaggerating. If it weren't for Laura, I don't know where I'd be today.

Laura gave me the greatest gift of all—the gift of kindness. She believed in me, and because she did, I began to believe in myself. She encouraged me to dream, and because she did, I began to have big dreams. Because of Laura, I got off the streets and I now have a beautiful family of my own. And I am teaching my children the same thing Laura taught me—that even a small act of kindness, like taking a hungry kid to lunch, can make all the difference in the world.

I know it did for me.

That's why I'm so proud of this book—because it's taking the great lesson I learned from Laura and sharing it with children everywhere. It's spreading the message that kindness counts. I was lucky enough to have Laura as my angel, but we all have angels out there, and we can all be angels to someone. I hope this book helps spread that message to everyone out there who really needs to hear it.

Thank you, Laura, and I love you.

Maurice Mazyck

SMALL ACTS OF KINDNESS

The theme of this book, and the life lesson from this story, is how small acts of kindness can have a major impact. It's a lesson most people would like their children to learn, and it's our hope this true story helps children understand it in an accessible way.

Laura and Maurice's hope by sharing their story is to inspire kindness. This story shows that an act of kindness doesn't have to be huge—actually, it can be very small. In fact, children can perform small acts of kindness every day, with their family, at school, and even out in their community. A small act might be giving a sibling a hug if they seem upset. It could be inviting the new child at school to eat lunch with them, or it could be donating old toys to a charity that serves less fortunate children. The holidays are a wonderful time to start talking about kindness. On top of talking about what gifts they want to get, you can also talk to your children about different ways they can *give*. You can begin to teach them that several small acts of kindness add up to a very giving year.

The beauty of Laura and Maurice's story is that it shows that even very small acts of kindness, like sharing a meal with someone, can be very meaningful. Kindness just happens. Here are a few inspiring ideas for how to get started on small acts of kindness:

• •

If you have a chart of family chores, add "kindness" to the list. Then check it off, or put a star or sticker, on the chart when your child does something kind. Just as we acknowledge setting the table or putting away laundry, it's important to acknowledge wonderful, kind behavior.

Once a month — at dinnertime on Sunday, for instance, or during a car trip — talk as a family about the one small kind act you each did and about what other acts of kindness you can do in the future.

At holiday or birthday time set aside time to do an act of kindness for someone outside your family. It could be shoveling snow for a neighbor, donating to a book drive, or giving one birthday present to a charity.

Start a Kindness Bear drive. Maurice gave Laura the one treasured possession he had: a small white bear. Encourage your child, or your child's class, to start a Kindness Bear campaign where each child donates a new stuffed animal to a charity that accepts them.

As the story of Laura and Maurice shows, one small act of kindness can mean the world to the child who receives that kindness.

For more ideas and to see how Laura champions small acts of kindness, visit aninvisiblethread.com.

LAURA AND MAURICE IN 1986

ONE SMALL ACT OF KINDNESS . . .

Donate a meal

Tell someone how
special they are

Share love

LAURA AND MAURICE TODAY

Help a neighbor

Pack lunch for
someone in need

Volunteer and give

Invite a new
friend to come over

. . . CAN CHANGE A LIFE FOREVER.

MAURICE AND HIS FAMILY